YOUR KNOWLEDGE HAS VALUE

- We will publish your bachelor's and
  master's thesis, essays and papers

- Your own eBook and book -
  sold worldwide in all relevant shops

- Earn money with each sale

Upload your text at www.GRIN.com
and publish for free

Bibliographic information published by the German National Library:

The German National Library lists this publication in the National Bibliography; detailed bibliographic data are available on the Internet at http://dnb.dnb.de .

Imprint:

Copyright © 2003 GRIN Verlag, Open Publishing GmbH
Print and binding: Books on Demand GmbH, Norderstedt Germany
ISBN: 9783640673360

Thomas Gräfe

The legal and moral legitimation of war in Shakespeare's 'Henry V'

GRIN Publishing

Thomas Gräfe

The legal and moral legitimation of war in Shakespeare's *Henry V*

Contents

The Legal and Moral Legitimation of War in Shakespeare's *Henry V*

I.   Shakespeare's Henry V: Glorification or criticism of war?
II.   The legitimation of war
II.1.   "jus ad bellum": The medieval concept of the "just war"
II.2   "jus in bello": Chivalric rules of behaviour in war
III.   Critical aspects in Henry V: The atrocity and futility of war
IV.   Patriotism and national stereotypes
V.   Conclusion

- In the Middle Ages war was, at least concerning political theory and rhetoric, governed by written and unwritten laws and conventions originating in Christian theology, philosophy and chivalric codes of honour.
  "jus ad bellum" = criteria deciding on the right to resort to war (e.g. a "just" cause)
  "jus in bello" = laws governing the conduct of war (e.g. how to treat prisoners of war)

- Henry, his knights and clergymen classify the campaign against France as a "just war" according to medieval legal and moral standards.

jus ad bellum	
just cause (= correcting wrongs)	I,2,esp. 33-121
declaration of war by a sovereign	II,4, 76-112
outcome of war as God's decision	II,2,189f; IV,4,132; IV,8,101-115
peace restored	V,2
jus in bello	
use of mercy	III,3,54
protection of civilians	III,6,103-108

- Emphasising English patriotism and heroism in the war did not make Shakespeare refrain from offering a critical or sceptical perspective on Henry's war. Adopting contemporary humanist ideas Shakespeare claims that ethical responsibilities should prevail over power politics. In many scenes the ambiguous and hypocritical character of the "just war" doctrine is revealed. In spite of its chivalrous rhetoric, it obviously fails to humanize warfare effectively. Examples:

Profane political motivations of the Church: I,1.
Henry's message to the inhabitants of Harfleur: III,3,1-43.
Motivations of the lower ranked knights and soldiers: III,2,10f.; III,2,26-49; IV,4.
Massacre of Agincourt: IV,6,36f.
Futility of war: V. Epilogue

<u>Literature</u>

Meron, Theodor, Bloody Constraint. War and Chivalry in Shakespeare, Oxford: University Press 1998.
Meron, Theodor, Henry's wars and Shakespeare's Laws. Perspectives on the Law of War in the Later Middle Ages, Oxford: Clarendon 1993.
Russell, Frederick H., The Just War in the Middle Ages, Cambridge: University Press 1975.

I.   Shakespeare's Henry V: Glorification or criticism of war?

While the first two plays of the Lancaster trilogy deal with domestic problems and power struggle during the War of the Roses (1455- 1485), Henry V is devoted to England's temporary successes in the Hundred Year's War (1337- 1453).

There are two opposing ways of interpreting Henry V. Either you can read it as an "affirmative play" (Iser, Shakespeare's Historien, p. 184.), which means that Shakespeare wanted to portray Henry V as an ideal ruler and to glorify the war against France as just and the victory as a great and heroic achievement. Unsurprisingly Henry V has frequently been used as a wartime propaganda play, esp. in the 20th century World Wars. (referring to the 1943 film version of Laurence Olivier: Holderness, Shakespeare Recycled, pp. 178- 210.) And there are speculations that the play had even been produced for this purpose as there are allusions to the English military expedition to Ireland of 1599 in the play. (V. Chor., 29-34.) Other critics argue that glorification of war, heroism, and patriotism are only forming a surface which is undermined by a sometimes more, sometimes less obvious critical or, at least, ambiguous undertone. (e.g. Goddard, The Meaning of Shakespeare, pp. 215- 268.) First let's have a look at the affirmative side.

II.   The legitimation of war

Henry's campaign against France (1415) is classified in the play as a "just war" on the basis of medieval religious and legal doctrines, in some cases mixed with Renaissance ideas. These laws and conventions dealing with the question of war can be divided in:

- "jus ad bellum" meaning the right to resort to war on the basis of legitimate moral reasons derived from Christian philosophy and theology.
- "jus in bello" referring to the law governing the conduct of war concerning questions like the treatment of prisoners of war, civilians etc. (Meron, Henry's wars, pp. 17- 46.)

II.1 "jus ad bellum": The medieval concept of the "just war"

In medieval Europe economic needs, power politics and personal ambitions of rulers were not acceptable as official grounds for warfare. According to Christian philosophy and theology, war should, at least officially, only serve a single aim: to restore God's prescribed order on earth if no other remedies could be found. In order to prove the justness of a war certain criteria of legitimation in both "jus ad bellum" and "jus in bello" had to be fulfilled (Russell, Just War.). A great deal of the language of war in the play is devoted to these criteria:

1.) The first necessity is to make clear that the enemy has broken fundamental laws, while the other warring party takes the part of God's worldly arm which corrects the wrongs and restores the order: In official situations Henry talks less about his personal war aims, but rather accuses the French of urging him to go to war. The Archbishop of Canterbury has to give his expert's opinion on the complex genealogical and legal situation. The result is that the Salian law does not apply to France so that Henry can justly claim his divine right to the French throne. Whereas the illegal usurpation of the French king must be brought to an end.

(I,2) **Film**

This message is repeated in the ultimatum the Duke of Exeter brings to the French court: "He wills you, in the name of God almighty,/ That you divest yourself, and lay apart/ The borrowed glories that by gift of heavn,/ By law of nature and nations belongs/ To him (…)" (II,4, 77-81.)

2.) War must be declared by a legitimate sovereign: Throughout the play Henry is praised as a perfect king and the society he rules over as a perfectly ordered commonwealth. The Archbishop of Canterbury compares it to a beehive in which every creature works according to its natural function. (I,2, 183-221.) The three traitors did not manage to overthrow the order and, when caught, they admit that they have done wrong. (II,2.) The king is no longer identified with his failings as a prince; he is now compared to his heroic ancestors like Edward the Black Prince. Bishop of Ely: "You are their heir; you sit upon their throne;/ The blood and courage that renowned them/ Runs in your veins (…) " (I,2, 117- 119.) Not only is Henry king by divine right, but, in contrast to Richard II., he is also praised as a charismatic, virtuous, and wise ruler – a king able to lead and win a war.

3.) The outcome of a war must be accepted as God's decision: Especially in the (English) court scenes, the role of God is in the centre of discussions and speeches on the conflict with France. Before the campaign is started, Henry makes clear to his noblemen that God is the decisive factor in the war: "Let us deliver our puissance into the hand's of God" (II,2, 189f.) He hopes for God's intervention in the battle of Aagincourt: "And how thou pleasest, God, dispose the day." (IV,2, 132.) "God's arm strike with us." (IV,3, 5.) And, in deed, the unexpected victory is ascribed to the power of divine intervention. Henry orders his soldiers to praise and thank God, and he says: "God, thy arm was here!/ And not to us, but to thy arm alone,/ Ascribe we all! When, without strategem,/ But in plain shock and even play of battle,/ Was ever known so great and little loss/ On one part and on the other? Take it, God/ For it is none but thine!" (IV,8, 101-115.)

4.) Peace must be restored and the defeated enemy must be integrated into order of the
victorious party: This requirement is fulfilled in the last scene by Henry's political marriage
with Katherine of France. This marriage is supposed to unite England and France under one
dynasty in order to "plant neighbourhood and Christian- like accord/ In their sweet bosoms,
that never war advance/ His bleeding sword twixt England and fair France." (V,2, 337- 339.)

II.2   "jus in bello": Chivalric rules of behaviour in war
Beside "justifying war on high moral grounds" (Campbell, Shakespeare's Histories, p. 259.),
what happened on the battlefield and in occupied territories was of some importance to the
"just war" doctrine as well. In a time in which soldiers usually lived off the land they invaded
it was very difficult to protect non-combatants and their property effectively. However,
abstaining from atrocities and following chivalric rules of behaviour in a war could contribute
to the image of a "just war". (Meron, Henry's wars, p. 122, 162f.) Usually this was expressed
by royal ordinances as it is done by Henry in act 3, scene 6: "(…) we give express charge that
in our marches through the country there be nothing compelled from the villages, nothing
taken but paid for; none of the French upbraided or abused in disdainful language (…)" (III,
6, 103- 107.) As an explicit warning that Henry does not tolerate violations of civilians and
their property, he orders the execution of his former companion Brandolph, who has stolen a
pix from a church. (III, 6, 98f, 103.) If you think of what happens at Harfleur and Agincourt,
it becomes clear that the king's ordinance of war is again rather a matter of rhetoric which can
be put aside if the situation affords it.

III.   Critical aspects in Henry V: The atrocity and futility of war
It cannot be overlooked that the rhetorical construction of a "just war" sounds rather
hypocritical. I picked out three examples which, I think, Shakespeare used to undermine the
credibility of the law of war rhetoric:

Even the institution which teaches the doctrine of "just war", namely the Church, seems to
have very profane reasons for encouraging the king to go to war. The conversation of the two
bishops right in the beginning of the play makes clear that they see the war as a welcome
distraction from political plans to deprive the Church of parts of its revenue. (I,1)

As mentioned above Henry's intention to be a just and merciful warlord is obviously
inconsistent. He threatens the inhabitants of Harfleur with all sorts of terrible war crimes, but

when they surrender he orders to "use mercy to them all". (III,3, 54.) On the one hand Henry protects the civilians by punishing the soldiers who have stolen and plundered. (III,6, 103ff.) On the other hand he decides to kill the prisoners when the course of the battle seems to make it necessary. (IV,6, 36f.) All in all the king's behaviour in war shows much more inconsistencies than his legitimacy of the war.

After Henry's speech on the battlefield (III,1), his heroic pathos is contrasted by the motivations of the simple and lower ranked soldiers. Justice, heroism and patriotism do not play the most important part in their discourses. Either they wish themselves back home (III,2, 10f.), or their main interest is plundering French villages and towns and pressing ransoms from prisoners of war. (III,2, 26- 49; IV,4.) When the king goes through the camp in disguise and asks Williams and Bates about the justness of the war, they answer that this is not their business. They are just prepared to obey the king and not to think about his politics: "That's more than we know (…) or more than we should seek after, for we know enough if we know we are the king's subjects." (IV,1,122-124)

But there are even some indicators that Henry is not really sure if his cause is just. In his prayer before the battle of Agincourt it becomes obvious that he fears to be punished by God for his father's usurpations of power: "O, not to-day, think not upon the fault/ My father made in compassing the crown!" (IV,1, 279f.)

The final words of the epilogue indicate the futility of Henry's war. Within a few years France will be lost again and all the bloodshed was in vain. (V. Epilogue)

IV.   patriotism and national stereotypes

Especially wartime interpretations of Henry V have stressed the patriotic or nationalist character of the play. By the pathetic and heroic language of war, Shakespeare allegedly wanted to strengthen English self- confidence and self- consciousness. (Holderness, Shakespeare Recycled, pp. 178- 210.) I would not use the term nationalism in this context because there is no identification with an English or even a British nation. On the contrary, there are conflicts in the English camp between the different nationalities (English, Scots, Welsh, Irish). But there is no doubt that a certain patriotic enthusiasm is present in the play.

It is formed by national stereotypes built on the contrast between the English and the French noblemen. The English noblemen are characterised as respectable, courageous, heroic, and reckless. Henry himself is a kind of role model for his subjects. He shows his determination: No compromise and no negotiations, either complete victory or total defeat: "No king of England, if not king of France" (II,2, 193.) He resigns to call for reinforcements giving the argument: "The fewer men, the greater share of honour." (IV,3, 22.), and he strengthens the confidence of his "inly ruminate" (IV. Chor., 24.) soldiers by rousing speeches before the battles. Obviously Henry's example and his speeches are successful. For instance, the Duke of York asks for the permission to lead the vanguard, although he knows he will be the first to be killed in battle: "My Lord, most humbly on my knee I beg/ The leading of the vaward." (IV,4, 129f.) In the end the English courage and bravery is rewarded by God with a glorious victory.

Throughout the play the French are portrayed as vain, arrogant, and over confident. This starts with the insulting present of the Dauphin (I,2, 247- 311.) and reaches a climax in the conversations of the French noblemen before the battle. (III,7.) They are superior in number, and think that they are going to win the battle anyway. They are less concerned with military affairs, but pride themselves with their armour, their horses, and their mistresses. The scene creates the impression of French decadence in a comic way because the audience already knows (or is likely to know) the outcome of the battle and can mock at the "confident and over- lusty French". (IV. Chor., 18.) Another aspect by which the French side is ridiculed is the use of the French language to create comic situations, when the daughter of king Charles tries to learn English (III,4.) and in Pistols conversation with his prisoner (IV,4.). As the French are lacking honour and courage, God punishes them with defeat and "shame, and eternal shame! Nothing but shame!" (IV,5, 11.)

V.   Conclusion

In conclusion, I think, it is not sufficient to read Henry V as a wartime propaganda play. Beside certain glorifications and English self- affirmation by the use of national stereotypes, Shakespeare also offers a critical perspective on Henry's war. He did not simply adopt the "just war" doctrine from medieval sources (Hall, Holinshed), but in many scenes he reveals its ambiguous and hypocritical character. The criteria of the "just war" are only fulfilled rhetorically, but they fail to humanize warfare effectively. (Meron, Bloody Constraint, p. 25, 202.)

VI. Literature

Campbell, L., Shakespeare's Histories. Mirrors of Elizabethan Policy, London: Methuen 1964, pp. 255- 305.

Goddard, Harold C., The Meaning of Shakespeare, Chicago 1951.

Holderness, G., Shakespeare Recycled. The Making of Historical Drama, New York: Harvester Wheatsheaf 1992, pp. 178- 210.

Iser, W., Shakespeare's Historien. Genesis und Geltung, Konstanz: Universitätsverlag 1988, pp. 183- 203.

Meron, Theodor, Bloody Constraint. War and Chivalry in Shakespeare, Oxford: University Press 1998.

Meron, Theodor, Henry's Wars and Shakespeare's Laws. Perspectives on the Law of War in the Later Middle Ages, Oxford: Clarendon 1993.

Russell, Frederick H., The Just War in the Middle Ages, Cambridge: University Press 1975.

YOUR KNOWLEDGE HAS VALUE

- We will publish your bachelor's and
  master's thesis, essays and papers

- Your own eBook and book -
  sold worldwide in all relevant shops

- Earn money with each sale

Upload your text at www.GRIN.com
and publish for free